Teacher on Break

Sarah Walsh

Presentation by *BookLeaf Publishing*

Web: www.bookleafpub.com

E-mail: info@bookleafpub.com

ISBN: 9789357440653

First edition 2023

DEDICATION

I would like to thank my mother, who always believed in me, no matter what dream I pursued.

The Beginning

Starting things is hard,
especially when
you are not confident,
you are inexperienced,
you are overly critical of yourself.
Beginnings are tough
because you have no direction,
Nothing behind you guiding you through this
new adventure.
Starting something new in writing,
is no exception.
Same lost feeling,
needing guidance,
looking for a sign.
In my classroom,
I can't count, how many times
I have told my students to just start writing,
writing anything,
to get a flow,
to just start
and the rest will follow.
It's just one of those things,
one of those things teachers say,
knowing it is for your good,
but also knowing,
that they wouldn't follow their own advice.

Sometimes though,
just following our own advice to the students,
actually helps us,
because a beginning is hard,
but if you just start writing,
writing anything,
eventually the rest does follow.

The Challenge Pt. 1

21 days of writing poetry,
that is what I signed up for.
Why would I do this to myself?
It was stupid,
writer's block is widely known for a reason,
it is real,
so why would I sign up for such a rigorous
writing challenge?
21 days, 21 poems,
no time to think,
just write.
This challenge may break me,
This challenge will change me.
This challenge won't complete itself.
I have faith,
I will find the motivation,
I will conquer this challenge.
21 poems, 21 days,
21 successes.

Anxiety

The impending doom
the feeling that is unending
overwhelming.

The dread over every interaction
over every mistake
it never goes away.

Some people
lucky people can just forget
they can just relax.

I envy those people
that just forget
and aren't haunted by the past.

A monster
my monster, unyielding
spreading doubts, spreading fears.

Someday
I will defeat
the doom, the monster.

Then I will know peace.

More Than Teaching

5

Teaching is more than many people ever know.

It is copious amounts of paperwork,
Sitting through Building Network Meetings,
Mentoring the lost,
Appeasing parents,
Analyzing data for every standard, unit, and
topic,
Counseling those in need,
Curriculum developing,
Buying supplies with your own money,
Coaching numerous sports,
Attending Staff Meetings,
Showing understanding for the students who
need more love,
Motivating all learners for all tasks,
Balancing all the hormones,
Inspiring students to become their best,
Student learning plans,
Regulating student emotions,
Tutoring those falling behind,
Mediating the many disagreements that
inevitably will happen,
Connecting your classroom to the outside world,
Explaining your choices to both students and
administrators,

Hearing out students that have no one else,
Attending professional development,
Listening to the stories on one wants to hear,
Answering emails,
Planning lessons that will be accessible for all
learners,
Advising clubs,
Participating in Professional Learning
Communities,
Evaluating students again and again,
Teaching new concepts in ways that engage
every student,
And most of all

Caring.

In the City

I am Anita,
but Anita is not me.
I created her out of boredom
for a digital city,
but she has become so much more.
She isn't real, but she is.
Everyday
time ticks down until freedom,
until Anita.

I crave the sound of the city starting up,
feel the rush of excitement
as I find out what I missed,
missed because of Sarah.
The city knows Anita,
but Sarah, they wouldn't l
Anita is my freedom,
Sarah is my reality.

I shut down, I hold my tongue.
I let things pass by,
holding onto them until I break,
But Anita speaks.
She knows no fear, just preservation.

She speaks her desires,
Shows her selfishness
and in turn is embraced by the city.
Anita is embraced by the city
ANITA is embraced by the city,
I am Anita,
but Anita is not me.

Christmas, I Guess

It's Christmas morning,
Usually, I would be running around,
Frantically packing,
Excitement bursting,
Ready to see my cousins,
Ready for good food and obnoxious bickering,
Ready for family.
This was always my day.
I got to be more than just my mother and me,
I belonged.

Not today.
This year, the families
will do their own thing.
This year, the families, more family than mine,
will celebrate on their own.
How nice,
for them.
My family has moved on,
Their happiness bringing tears,
Tears or joy
Tears of loneliness
Tears for the sake of tears.
I thought this feeling would shake
as I got older,

as I dated,
as I spread my wings,
But some feelings only worsen over time.
rooting into your very soul
twisting, controlling
becoming a piece of your core
so deep, you will never escape.

It didn't even matter.
The not so Christmas Christmas,
Never would have been anyway.
A blizzard and a broken furnace would have
stood in my way,
even if we planned to do things
the old way.
Christmas will never be the same.
Christmas is just another day.

Sitting Still

If I sit still,
Maybe this moment can stretch
into more.
Two weeks seems so long,
but it is not.
Breaks always paralyze me.
I must sit still and allow time to slowly wash
over me,
The more I do,
The quicker time will move,
and my salvation will come to an end.

Sitting Too Still

Days crawl by,
My stillness letting every moment linger,
I relish the stillness,
As the monstrous thoughts
Turn my salvation into a prison.

What I once yearned for,
Becomes involuntary.
I am paralyzed,
Stuck sitting still,
Even from the things I want to do.
All I wanted before, turned into a prison.
Break is only two weeks,
I need to celebrate each moment,
Make the most of every minute, but
I can't,
Even if I want to,
Lose myself in friends and family,
I am stuck sitting still.

I wanted to sit still
And now,
I am stuck sitting still.

Writing Challenge

I love to write
I really do
so why has this experience
been so difficult?
Why
do I sit thinking and thinking
until I make myself sick
about writing
only to never start?
I enjoy writing
so this
should be a welcomed retreat
my highlight of the day
my way to get out of frustration.
Why
can't it be that
is it the added pressure
the looming deadline?
Maybe it is the competition
will I be good enough
will I make my believers proud?
Why
is it that when you bring the outside world
into what you love

It ruins it?
Will
writing once again be my comfort place
when this is over
or will this writer's block linger
and I have destroyed
my solace?

Lean and Clean Machine

I dream of her,
the perfect version of me.
She cleans as she goes,
never leaving a mess behind.
She cooks every meal from scratch,
never letting fast food touch her lips.
She finds time for at least a quick workout
everyday,
even when she is tired.
She picks up a book,
and her television set remains cold.
She checks in on her family every week,
and not just her mother, everyone.
She folds the laundry as soon as it is done,
and wouldn't know the smell that comes after
days of forgetting it.
She prepares her lunches on Sundays for the
whole week,
and wouldn't have to go hungry most days.
She keeps a budget,
never giving into the impulse to buy more than
she needs.
She can say no,
never letting the outside world weigh her down.
She walks her dogs everyday,

even when it seems like the day has been a little
too long.
She grades work the day it is turned in by her
students,
and doesn't let it pile up.

But most importantly,
She never loses her cool,
always the model of patience and kindness.
I dream of her.

Different Languages

My love language is
acts of service.
Help me
with something I struggle with
and I am yours.
Do something menial
that I dread
and it will feel as if
 you moved heaven and earth
just to make me happy.
It doesn't take much,
small things,
small things that show you are thinking of me.

Your love language is
physical touch.
Contact,
more contact,
and even more contact,
is what you crave.
A touch of the arm,
cuddling during movies,
tickle fights around the house,
that is what fills you,
makes you complete,

shows you that I care.

We speak different languages.
I shrink away,
you shut down,
communication stops,
frustration grows,
and we pull apart.
We speak different languages,
and that
may just be
what breaks us.

Reading Paradox

I love reading,
getting lost in a book,
in a kingdom that will never exist,
in drama I would dread in real life,
in a love story that is predictable and safe,
so why
do I not pick up a book at home?
Why does reading seem like the last option,
only when all technology has failed,
I have completed every puzzle in my house,
and completed the impossible task of organizing
my life?
If I love reading so much,
why does it never win?
I will try so hard to be a good reader.
I will set timers,
pick great books,
even find audiobooks for my drives,
but after a couple weeks,
the tv beckons,
the computer calls,
the phone roars.
But my books,
sitting in the corner,
silently,

not commanding my attention,
not screaming out for love,
not demanding anything of me.
For these reasons,
I love books,
But for these same reasons,
I forget about them,
leaving them cast away for more shiny things.

Notifications

Nothing ruins a break
faster than a group chat.
We all dread that first single notification,
seeing everyone else,
knowing the imminent bombardment
is soon to begin.
Ding, beep, buzz,
it doesn't matter what sound,
just the frequency.
Once one comes,
then two, then three, then four,
a flood of interruptions,
loud,
even when silenced,
intruding on your life,
consuming.

Notification anxiety
is real.
Its relentless,
unyielding,
intrusive.
Each notification,
lurches my emotions
to the surface,

until I feel like I will burst.

I should feel
wanted,
loved,
needed.
Instead I feel overwhelmed.
Am I a freak,
can I just not deal,
is my anxiety really that bad,
or is it normal
to descend into despair
with that first group chat notification?

Water Bottles

"A water bottle is not your personality",
is something I heard a while ago,
that has really stuck with me.
Why can't a water bottle be your personality?
Thinking back,
a younger version of me,
would agree,
while arguing how ridiculous the concept
sounds,
but in today's world,
it makes sense.
A water bottle can tell us so much,
the market for them has thrived,
for good reason.
A water bottle can show consciousness,
preference,
habits,
awareness.
It can hint at your socio-economic status,
suggest your style,
declare your health state,
and show if you follow the crowd.
A water bottle can be your personality,
it can tell the world all about you,
if you let it.

Habits

I have always found it
fascinating,
how habits work.
66 days,
that is all it takes,
to change whatever about yourself,
that you don't love.

Seems easy enough.
66 days,
just over two months,
but that only works with perfection.
You have to be on for 66 days,
staying motivated,
for 66 days,
staying on track,
for 66 days,
doing the one thing that has always escaped you,
for 66 days.
Seems simple enough,
as if we have just been handed
the keys to the universe,
the secret,
to a happy life.

Habits are fascinating,
once you manage
to break through those 66 days,
a new you emerges,
better than before,
embodying what you have always lacked.
It took 66 days to start becoming that new
person,
yet that new person can be destroyed in just a
few days.
Bad habits
are fun, easy to relapse into.
Good habits
take commitment, quick to disappear.

The Impending Return

I don't want to go back,
I don't want the break to end.
I understand break is longer for us than most,
I get it,
I really do,
but it still isn't long enough.
I need more
More time, more calm.
I love my students,
But calm and students can't co-exist.

The Game

You just lost the game,
I'm sorry,
but a student
just ruined my thirteen year streak,
right before break started.
Since I lost the game,
after such a high score,
I can't seem to stop thinking about it.
Since then,
I have lost the game at least eight times more
and
since I have lost the game,
I needed you to as well.

Older, Not Wiser

Every year,
I retreat into myself more,
hide more away,
become more self-dependent.
I use to think,
it would get easier,
as I got older,
to figure things out,
but here I am,
older,
none the wiser,
and just as confused.
Still lost,
wandering through life,
Stumbling to find my home,
Maybe someday,
when I am older,
things will be easier to figure out.

The Challenge Pt. 2

Days tick by
and I am still not done.
I am still writing,
still participating in this writing challenge.
Challenges are appropriately named,
fitting,
I never really thought about it.
We dress up different things with the word challenge,
implying it may be fun,
something outside the normal,
but sometimes we forget,
or rather I forget,
they are called challenges for a reason.
They disrupt our norm,
making us be more if we wish to succeed,
throwing us into pits of despair when we fail,
but either way changing us.

21 days of writing,
no time to flounder,
no time to hesitate,
no time for second guessing,
no time for my over-analyzing, compulsive, worrying
mind,
this challenge has changed me,
for the better.

There is Always Garlic

There is something about cooking,
throwing random ingredients
into a pan
no measurements
no recipe
no rules,
just you and the food.
It is freeing
to lead with your heart,
to feel what is right.
Cooking is an escape,
the stress of everything,
melts in the pan,
marrying the flavors into something new,
delicious.
And when it doesn't work out,
there is always garlic
to save the day.

The Night Before

The night before return
is always full of emotion.
I yell
because I am frustrated
because I am mad
because I am nervous.

The night before return
is hard for teachers too.
The pit in your stomach
grows deeper and deeper,
anticipating
the new day
the new challenges
the new opportunities.

The night before return
is always hard.
I struggle
because I am frustrated
because I am mad
because I am nervous.

www.ingramcontent.com/pod-product-compliance
Lightning Source LLC
Chambersburg PA
CBHW070724160726
48003CB00006BA/2366